W9-BLP-001

LIVING LANGUAGE®

Say It By Signing

Elaine Costello, Ph.D.

Illustrated by
**Lois A. Lehman
Linda C. Tom**

LIVING LANGUAGE,
A RANDOM HOUSE COMPANY
NEW YORK

Acknowledgments

Special thanks to the Living Language team: Lisa Alpert, Elizabeth Bennett, Helen Tang, Elyse Tomasello, Christopher Warnasch, Christopher Medellín, Zviezdana Verzich, Suzanne McGrew, Pat Ehresmann, and Linda Schmidt.

Published by Living Language, A Random House Company, New York, New York.
Living Language is a member of the Random House Information Group.

Random House, Inc. New York, Toronto, London, Sydney, Auckland

www.livinglanguage.com

Living Language and colophon are registered trademarks of Random House, Inc.

Printed in the United States of America

Design by Elaine Costello

Library of Congress Cataloging-in-Publication Data available upon request.

ISBN 0-609-81054-5

10 9 8 7 6 5 4 3 2 1

First Edition

Table of Contents

Introduction

Welcome!

You are about to learn a fascinating language that is unlike any other language in the world. Instead of a language of sounds like all spoken languages, American Sign Language is a visual language formed by organized hand gestures, movements, and facial expressions.

Who Uses American Sign Language?

American Sign Language (ASL) is the native language of about 400,000 people in the United States. Most of the native users are deaf, but some native users are the hearing children and other relatives of Deaf* people. A *native* language is a the first language a person learns, and it is learned naturally through interaction with other users.

Approximately 600,000 hearing and Deaf people use ASL or some form of sign language on a daily basis. Relatives, neighbors, and co-workers of Deaf people are among the hearing people who learn sign language. Some people are able to learn ASL as a second language and become proficient enough to use it as fluently as native signers.

Deaf is spelled with a capital *D* when referring to members of the Deaf community.

Although ASL has its roots in French Sign Language, it is unique to North America. Most countries have their own sign language with their own signs and structure. No universal sign language exists. Do not misunderstand sign language as a word-for-word translation of English, either. It has its own word order and structure, often very different from spoken English.

Conceptual Signing

Signs are the phonological units of ASL. Signs cannot be paired one-to-one with English words; instead signs represent concepts. Usually English words are used to *gloss,* or represent, the meaning of a sign because ASL has no written form. When English glosses are written to represent signs, they appear in capital letters. Sometimes a "string" of signs is necessary to express a concept that requires only one English word to say. For example, the two signs NOT-YET and DECIDE are signed for the concept "undecided," which is expressed in one English word. Conversely, ASL is efficient in that a single sign, SIX-MONTHS, is used for the concept "six months," which requires two English words.

Getting Started in Sign

This book will introduce you to a basic sign vocabulary, sufficient to converse in sign language with Deaf people. The format of this book is unique in that basic grammatical rules of the structure of ASL are presented in easy-to-learn sections, immediately followed by examples that clearly demonstrate the application of those rules. The final chapter of this book provides an opportunity for you to practice sign vocabulary in phrases, an intermediary step to signing sentences. The "drill" format of these exercises is similar to the techniques used sucessfully in teaching English in English-as-a-Second-Language courses. The video-tape that accompanies this book reinforces ASL's essential grammar and shows you how to use ASL in connected discourse.

This book and the accompanying videotape will get you started in ASL, but in order to become profi-cient, make sure you take advantage of every oppor-tunity to meet and mingle with Deaf people. Use every opportunity to try out your signs so that you learn to use them fluently.

The good news is that Deaf people will be able to communicate with you even if you use the signs you learn in this book in the sequence of English sen-tences. Deaf people know both ASL and English, and when they realize you are signing in an English word order, they will *code switch* to accommodate your signing style.

If you are trying to sign a concept, but you don't know a sign, you can always spell out the English word using *fingerspelling*. Fingerspelling is the letter-by-letter spelling of English words using the hand-shapes of the American Manual Alphabet (see pages 9-10). Usually fingerspelling is used for words for which there is no sign, such as proper names and technical terms.

Signs Have Variations

ASL is a living language and, like all languages, it changes over time. As technology and concepts come into vogue, ASL users develop new signs that become part of the language. Historically, for ease and speed of formation, signs that used to be formed with two hands are now formed with one hand. Signs have also moved inward toward the center of the chest where they can be observed more easily.

ASL also accommodates regional variations. Signs are developed by communities of users as necessary for communication. As Deaf people travel and use their signs with other Deaf people, the variations become apparent. As you learn sign language, don't be dismayed to see more than one sign for the same concept. These variations are a product of a living, growing language.

Enjoy your experience in learning sign language, have fun with it, and don't forget to practice with native users. Good luck.

A Guide to Using This Book

The signs in this book are arranged in the order that they appear in the accompanying videotape. Each part in the book corresponds with a lesson in the videotape. The signs are best learned by viewing the video and then using this book with line drawings to help recall how the signs are made.

Many of the signs in the book may be conceptually translated with more than one English word. These alternate glosses are given with each illustration. All of the glosses are listed alphabetically in the index at the end of the book. The index is helpful to search for a particular sign.

Each entry in this book consists of a line drawing of the sign and a description of each of the four parts of the sign. Look at the four parts of the sign NOT.

NOT
Handshape: 10
Orientation: palm left
Location: under chin
Movement: forward
Note: Sign may be accompanied with a negative headshake.

Handshape. When a sign is formed with only one hand, the handshape is given for the dominant hand (i.e., usually the right hand). When two hands are used, the handshape for the dominant hand is given first separated by a colon from the handshape for the other hand. The notations RH for right hand and LH for left hand are used, presuming that the right hand is the dominant hand for the signer. Left-handed signers should reverse the directions in the sign as necessary. If the handshape of either hand changes during the formation of the sign, that change is note here, too (e.g., A changes to S : open).

Most of the handshapes are the taken from the American Manual Alphabet and from numbers. Some handshapes are unique or are modifications. Some of these handshapes are as follows:

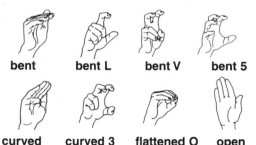

bent	bent L	bent V	bent 5

curved	curved 3	flattened O	open

Orientation. The direction that the palm faces when making a sign can make a difference in the meaning of the sign. The palm orientation is described as follows: right, left, up, down, in, forward. The palm orientation is given for the initial position when beginning to execute the sign. The position of the hands with one another is also described in this section.

Location. "Neutral space" is indicated for most of the signs. This refers to the space just in front of the lower chest where the hands most naturally can move and where the receiver's eye can most easily see the signs. About 90 percent of all signs are formed in this location. In this section, the initial location (e.g., thumb on chin) indicates where the sign begins prior to any movements.

Movement. The arrows on the drawings show the movement used in executing the sign. The text also describes the movement and tells the ending position including the location and palm orientation.

Note. The "note" section is used for indication of non-manual cues, if necessary; for variations in sign formation that are permissible; and for other information that may help you use the sign appropriately.

Glossary

conceptual signing – choosing to use a sign based on the concept being expressed and not the equivalent English word

fingerspelling – the spelling out of each letter of an English word by using the American Manual Alphabet

gloss – an English word that represents the same concept as a sign; glosses are usually written with capital letters

iconic – signs that look like an aspect of its referent

manual communication – a generic term used to refer to any communication formed on the hands

non-manual cue – a facial expression or other body language that contributes to the meaning of a sign

referent – the person or thing being discussed

sign – a meaningful gesture that represents a concept and can be described by its handshape, palm orientation, location, and movement

signer – the person using sign language

Part One
Meeting Old Friends

Signing Space

The area of the body used for the purpose of form-ing signs is called the signing space. The signing space extends form the top of the head to the upper hip, and as wide as the shoulders. The signing space is indicated in the boxed area of this illustration.

Signing Space

Only a few signs are formed on top of the head, and only a few signs are formed at the waist or lower. Likewise, very few signs are formed at the sides of the signing space. Here are some examples of signs formed at the extreme edges of the signing space.

RABBIT

Handshape: H : H
Orientation: palms back
Location: each side of top of head
Movement: bend fingers down with a double movement

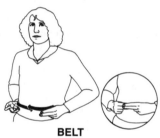

BELT

Handshape: H : H
Orientation: palms in, fingers pointing toward each other
Location: each side of waist
Movement: bring extended fingers toward each other and overlap in front of waist

CRACKER

Handshape: A
Orientation: palm up
Location: near elbow of bent left arm
Movement: tap palm side of RH on left elbow with a repeated movement

LEG

Handshape: open
Orientation: palm left, fingers pointing down
Location: right thigh
Movement: pat right thigh with a double movement

Neutral Space

Most signs are formed in front of the chest in an area called neutral space. In neutral space, the hands are comfortably held and signs are easily formed and viewed. Here are some one-handed and two-handed signs formed in neutral space.

LIKE

Handshape: curved changes to 8
Orientation: palm in
Location: neutral space
Movement: pull the hand forward while closing the thumb to the middle finger forming an 8 hand

FURNITURE

Handshape: F : F
Orientation: palms forward, fingers pointing up
Location: neutral space
Movement: shake both hands with a short side-to-side movement

SOON

Handshape: H : H
Orientation: palms angled toward each other
Location: neutral space
Movement: slide the side of the right middle finger back and forth on the side of the left index finger

WAIT

Handshape: 5 : 5
Orientation: both palms apart and up, fingers curved and pointing forward
Location: neutral space
Movement: wiggle fingers

Change Over Time

Through use, over time, changes in the formation of signs has occurred to make signs easier to form and easier to view. Signs have become more centralized, moving toward the neutral space in front of the body. Signs formerly made with two hands are now made with one hand. Signs frequently used together have assimilated into a single compound sign, as discussed in a future section. Signs borrowed from other languages have been added to the lexicon of sign language. Signs have been added for new concepts and technology to meet the needs of the users.

COW (two hands)

Handshape: Y : Y
Orientation: both palms forward
Location: thumbs touching each side of the head
Movement: twist wrists forward

COW (one hand)

Handshape: Y
Orientation: palm forward
Location: thumb touching side of the head
Movement: twist wrist forward

DECIDE, DETERMINE (THINK + JUDGE)
Handshape: 1 changes to F : F
Orientation: RH palm down; LH palm right
Location: RH on forehead; LH neutral space
Movement: bring right finger down to near left hand while changing to F hand; then move both hands downward

ROOM (borrowed from English)
Handshape: R : R
Orientation: palms facing each other
Location: hands apart in neutral space
Movement: bend wrists, moving left palm near body and RH somewhat forward, both palms facing in

COMPUTER (new technology)
Handshape: C
Orientation: palm forward
Location: thumb near the crook of the bent left arm
Movement: move the RH in an arc to the left wrist

Changing One Aspect of a Sign

Each sign has four parts, or aspects, that help distinguish it from other signs. If one of those four parts changes, the sign may become another sign or may become meaningless. The parts of a sign are as follows: 1) handshape; 2) palm orientation; 3) location; 4) movement. The following three signs all have a five handshape but the other parts of the sign change causing a new sign to be formed.

FINE

Handshape: 5
Orientation: palm left; fingers pointing up
Location: thumb on chest
Movement: tap thumb on chest with repeated movement

COLOR

Handshape: 5
Orientation: palm in; fingers pointing up
Location: near chin
Movement: wiggle fingers

AREA

Handshape: 5
Orientation: palm down; fingers pointing forward
Location: neutral space
Movement: move hand in a flat circle

More Than One Handshape

Not all signs have only one handshape or location. Many signs begin in one location with one handshape and then move to another location while changing to another handshape. Here are some examples of signs made with one hand that change handshape while changing location.

PRETTY, BEAUTIFUL, LOVELY
Handshape: 5 changes to flattened O
Orientation: palm in
Location: in front of face
Movement: move hand in a circle in front of face, closing fingers to thumb in front of chin

THROW, THROW AWAY
Handshape: S changes to 5
Orientation: palm in
Location: neutral space
Movement: forward and down while changing to 5 hand

Fingerspelling

Fingerspelling is the spelling out of each letter of an English word using the American Manual Alphabet. Usually proper names and things for which there is no sign, or for which the sign is not known, are fingerspelled. Words are spelled out smoothly, letter by letter, in front of the shoulder. For double letters, bounce your hand slightly to indicate that the letter is repeated. Here are the letters of the manual alphabet.

American Manual Alphabet

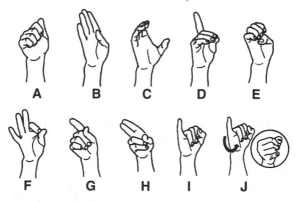

A   B   C   D   E

F   G   H   I   J

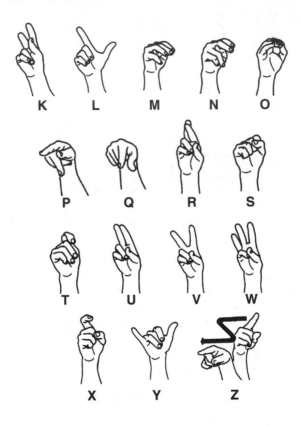

Personal Pronouns

In sign language, personal pronouns are formed by indexing or pointing to the person or thing. If the person or thing is not within view, a place in space can be set up and identified for that person or thing. Then that location can be pointed to. Here are the signs for personal pronouns used when the referent can be seen.

I, ME

Handshape: 1
Orientation: palm right, index finger pointing in
Location: near chest
Movement: touch the chest with the extended index finger

HE, SHE, IT

Handshape: 1
Orientation: palm down, index finger pointing toward referent
Location: neutral space
Movement: jab index finger toward referent

YOU (singular)

Handshape: 1
Orientation: palm down, index finger pointing forward
Location: neutral space
Movement: jab index finger forward toward referent

WE

Handshape: 1
Orientation: palm down
Location: right side of chest
Movement: swing hand in an arc in front of chest to touch left side of chest

YOU (plural)

Handshape: 1
Orientation: palm down, index finger pointing forward
Location: neutral space
Movement: swing the index finger from pointing forward in an arc to the right toward referents

THEY, THEM

Handshape: 1
Orientation: palm down, index finger pointing toward referents
Location: neutral space
Movement: swing index finger in an arc toward referents

Possessive Pronouns

Possessive pronouns are pronouns showing ownership. In sign language, possessive pronouns are formed in a similar manner to personal pronouns, except the open hand is directed toward the person or thing being discussed instead of indexing. The following signs are used for possessive pronouns when the referent is within view.

MY, MINE

Handshape: open
Orientation: palm in
Location: near chest
Movement: bring palm in against chest

HIS, HER, ITS

Handshape: open
Orientation: palm toward referent
Location: neutral space
Movement: push hand toward referent

YOUR (singular)

Handshape: open
Orientation: palm forward
Location: neutral space
Movement: push hand forward toward referent

US

Handshape: U
Orientation: palm right, fingers pointing up
Location: near right side of chest
Movement: swing hand from the right side of the chest in an arc to the left side of the chest

OUR

Handshape: curved
Orientation: palm left
Location: thumb on right side of chest
Movement: swing the hand in an arc to the left side of the chest, ending with palm facing right and little finger on chest

YOUR (plural)

Handshape: open
Orientation: palm forward toward referent
Location: neutral space
Movement: move hand in an arc to the right toward referents

THEIR

Handshape: open
Orientation: palm toward referent
Location: neutral space
Movement: push hand in an arc toward referents

Reflexive Pronouns

Reflexive pronouns are used for emphasis. In sign language, reflexive pronouns are formed by directing the extended thumb toward the person or thing being discussed. Here are the signs for reflexive pronouns.

MYSELF

Handshape: A
Orientation: palm left
Location: thumb near chest
Movement: tap the thumb against the chest with a double movement

HIMSELF, HERSELF, ITSELF

Handshape: A
Orientation: palm left
Location: neutral space
Movement: push thumb toward referent

YOURSELF

Handshape: A
Orientation: palm left
Location: neutral space
Movement: push thumb forward toward referent

OURSELVES

Handshape: A
Orientation: palm left
Location: right side of chest
Movement: move the hand in an arc from the right to touch the left side of the chest

YOURSELVES

Handshape: A
Orientation: palm left
Location: neutral space
Movement: move the hand in an arc to the right toward referents

THEMSELVES

Handshape: A
Orientation: palm left
Location: neutral space
Movement: push thumb in an arc toward referents

Common Greetings

The following signs are common expressions that you will need in everyday polite conversation. Be sure to use appropriate facial expression as you form the signs. Facial expression is a non-manual cue and serves as an integral part of the meaning of signs. Non-manual cues serve a role similiar to the role that vocal inflection serves in spoken languages.

HELLO, HI

Handshape: B
Orientation: palm forward; fingers pointing up
Location: right side of forehead
Movement: outward to the right

PLEASE

Handshape: open
Orientation: palm in
Location: chest
Movement: circular movement

THANK YOU

Handshape: open
Orientation: palm in; fingers pointing up toward mouth
Location: in front of mouth
Movement: forward

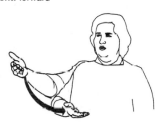

WELCOME, YOU'RE WELCOME

Handshape: curved
Orientation: palm up
Location: in front of right side of body
Movement: swing arm to the left in front of body

GOOD-LUCK

Handshape: open changes to 10
Orientation: palm in; fingers pointing up
Location: fingers on mouth
Movement: forward toward referent while changing to
a 10 hand

GOOD-BYE

Handshape: open changes to bent
Orientation: palm forward
Location: neutral space
Movement: bend the fingers up and down

SORRY

Handshape: A
Orientation: palm in
Location: chest
Movement: repeated circular movement

EXCUSE ME, FORGIVE ME

Handshape: open : open
Orientation: palms facing, RH above LH
Location: neutral space
Movement: brush right fingers across left palm with double movement

NO

Handshape: thumb, index finger, and middle finger extended changes to fingers closed to thumb
Orientation: palm forward
Location: neutral space
Movement: close fingers to thumb with double movement

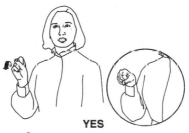

YES

Handshape: S
Orientation: palm forward
Location: neutral space
Movement: bend wrist down with double movement

OKAY

Handshape: O changes to K
Orientation: palm forward
Location: neutral space
Movement: without moving arm, hand changes to K

Gender

Many signs indicate whether they refer to a male or a female by the location in which they are formed. Male nouns are traditionally formed near the forehead, and female nouns are formed near the chin. The following signs for family members demonstrate this grammatical principle. The sign for PARENTS is formed in both the male and female locations because both a male and female person are included.

PARENTS

Handshape: 5
Orientation: palm left; fingers pointing up
Location: thumb touching right side of chin
Movement: move thumb up to touch right temple

BOY

Handshape: O changes to flattened C
Orientation: palm left
Location: thumb side on right side of forehead
Movement: close fingers and thumb together with a double movement

GIRL

Handshape: 10
Orientation: palm down
Location: thumb on lower right cheek
Movement: brush toward chin with a double movement

MAN, GENTLEMAN, MALE

Handshape: A changes to 5
Orientation: palm left
Location: thumb on right side of forehead
Movement: hand changes to 5 hand while moving down to touch thumb on chest

WOMAN, FEMALE, LADY

Handshape: A changes to 5
Orientation: palm left
Location: thumb on chin
Movement: hand changes to 5 hand while moving down to touch thumb on chest

DAUGHTER

Handshape: 10 changes to open : open
Orientation: RH palm right; LH palm up
Location: RH thumb on cheek; LH neutral space
Movement: RH thumb brushes down cheek, then changes to open hand while moving down, ending with back of right arm cradled in bent left arm

SON

Handshape: flattened C changes to open : open
Orientation: RH palm left; LH palm up
Location: RH thumb side on right side of forehead; LH neutral space
Movement: RH moves down, ending with back of right arm cradled in bent left arm

MOTHER, MAMA, MOM, MOMMY

Handshape: 5
Orientation: palm left
Location: thumb on chin
Movement: tap thumb twice on chin

FATHER, DAD, DADDY, PAPA

Handshape: 5
Orientation: palm left
Location: thumb on forehead
Movement: tap thumb twice on forehead

GRANDMOTHER

Handshape: 5
Orientation: palm left
Location: thumb on chin
Movement: hand moves forward in double arc

GRANDFATHER

Handshape: 5
Orientation: palm left
Location: thumb on forehead
Movement: hand moves forward in double arc

BROTHER

Handshape: flattened C changing to 1 : 1
Orientation: palm down
Location: thumb side on right side of forehead
Movement: hand changes to 1 hand while moving down

SISTER

Handshape: 10 changing to 1 : 1
Orientation: palm down
Location: thumb side on lower right cheek
Movement: hand changes to 1 hand while moving down

NIECE

Handshape: N
Orientation: palm left
Location: near right side of chin
Movement: twist hand forward and back

NEPHEW

Handshape: N
Orientation: palm left
Location: near the right temple
Movement: twist hand forward and back

COUSIN (male)

Handshape: C
Orientation: palm left
Location: near right temple
Movement: shake hand

COUSIN (female)

Handshape: C
Orientation: palm left
Location: near right side of chin
Movement: shake hand

Questions

Non-manual cues are an important part of asking questions in sign language. The body tends to lean forward and a quizzical expression is on the face, such as raising the eyebrows. Often the last sign is held a little longer. A question mark may be drawn in the air either before or after a question. The question why is often used as a preface to a statement for emphasis. Here are some signs used as questions.

WHAT

Handshape: 1 : open
Orientation: RH palm left, index finger in left palm; LH palm up
Location: neutral space
Movement: bring right index finger down across left palm

WHO

Handshape: 1
Orientation: palm in, index finger pointing toward lips
Location: in front of mouth
Movement: move finger in small circle in front of lips

WHICH

Handshape: 10 : 10
Orientation: palms apart facing each other
Location: neutral space
Movement: move hands up and down with an alternating
movement

WHY

Handshape: bent hand changes to Y
Orientation: palm in
Location: right side of forehead
Movement: hand moves forward while changing to Y hand

WHEN

Handshape: 1 : 1
Orientation: palms facing, fingers pointing toward each other
Location: neutral, RH above LH
Movement: move right index finger in circular movement
around and landing on left index finger

HOW MUCH

Handshape: curved : curved
Orientation: palms apart facing each other
Location: neutral space
Movement: move hands apart a short distance

WHERE

Handshape: 1
Orientation: palm forward
Location: neutral space
Movement: shake finger from side to side with a double movement

HOW

Handshape: curved : curved
Orientation: palms facing in opposite directions, knuckles touching
Location: chest
Movement: twist fingers up ending with palms up

HOW MANY
Handshape: S changes to 5
Orientation: palm up
Location: neutral space
Movement: flick fingers open quickly
Note: This sign may be made with two hands.

QUESTION, QUESTION MARK
Handshape: 1 changes to X changes back to 1
Orientation: palm forward, finger pointing forward
Location: in front of right shoulder
Movement: move finger downward with a curving movement while bending index finger and then extending it again

Person Marker

In English, a suffix is added to some words to change the meaning of someone's occupation or identity. For example, the suffix *-ist* can be added to *art* to form *artist*, or *-er* can be added to *teach* to become *teacher*. Similarly in sign language, an inflection referred to as the person marker can be added to signs to form signs for occupations or identities. The person marker is formed after the base sign by bringing both open hands downward along the sides of the body.

PERSON MARKER

Handshape: open : open
Orientation: palms facing each other
Location: in front of each side of body
Movement: downward along sides of the body

TEACH, EDUCATE, INSTRUCT

Handshape: flattened O : flattened O
Orientation: RH palm left; LH palm right
Location: near each side of the hear
Movement: move hands forward in a short double movement

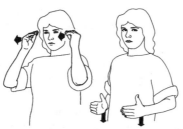

TEACHER

Compound sign: TEACH + person marker

ACT, DRAMA, PERFORM, PLAY, SHOW, THEATER
Handshape: A : A
Orientation: palms facing each other
Location: thumbs touching each side of chest
Movement: downward with alternating circular movements

ACTOR, ACTRESS, PERFORMER
Compound Sign: ACT + person marker

CAMERA
Handshape: L : bent L
Orientation: palms facing each other
Location: near each side of the head
Movement: bend the right index finger down

PHOTOGRAPHER
Compound Sign: CAMERA + person marker

WRITE, EDIT
Handshape: baby O : open
Orientation: RH palm down; LH palm up
Location: neutral space
Movement: RH moves with a wiggling movement from heel
to fingers of left palm

WRITER, AUTHOR, EDITOR
Compound Sign: WRITE + person marker

SELL, MERCHANDISE, RETAIL, SALE
Handshape: flattened O : flattened O
Orientation: both palms down
Location: neutral space
Movement: bend wrists up and down

SALESCLERK, MERCHANT, SALESPERSON, SELLER
Compound Sign: SELL + person marker

SERVE, SERVICE, WAIT ON
Handshape: open : open
Orientation: both palms up
Location: apart in front of each side of body
Movement: forward and back with an alternating movement

WAITER, WAITRESS, SERVER
Compound Sign: SERVE + person marker

ARMY

Handshape: A : A
Orientation: both palms in, right hand above left hand
Location: right side of chest
Movement: tap both palms against chest with a double movement

SOLDIER
Compound Sign: ARMY + person marker

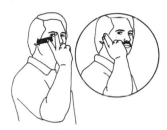

HAIRCUT

Handshape: V : V
Orientation: both palms down
Location: on each side of the neck
Movement: open and close fingers while moving fingers
back along hairline

BARBER, BEAUTICIAN, HAIR STYLIST
Compound Sign: HAIRCUT + person marker

LAW

Handshape: L : open
Orientation: palms facing each other
Location: neutral space
Movement: tap right palm on left palm, first near the
fingers and then on the heel

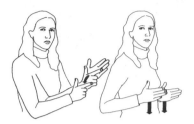

LAWYER, ATTORNEY
Compound Sign: LAW + person marker

LEARN
Handshape: 5 changes to flattened O : open
Orientation: RH palm down; LH palm up
Location: neutral space; right fingers on left palm
Movement: RH hand moves upward to right side of forehead while changing to flattened O

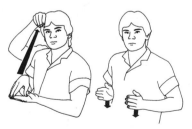

STUDENT, PUPIL
Compound Sign: LEARN + person marker

Part Two

Going Out With Friends

Iconic Signs

It is helpful to think of many signs as picture-like, or iconic. Although the signs are not truly iconic, there is a perceived relationship between the sign and its referent that assists in helping to remember the sign. For some signs, the iconic element is global; that is, the sign shows the shape of the referent. In some signs, the sign may show a feature of the referent, and in other signs, the sign may show what the referent does.

TELEPHONE, PHONE
(global: shape of telephone receiver)
Handshape: Y
Orientation: palm left
Location: near right side of face
Movement: bring palm side of RH to right cheek, little finger near mouth and thumb near ear

CAT
(feature: cat's whiskers)
Handshape: 5 changes to F
Orientation: palm left, fingers pointing up
Location: near side of the mouth
Movement: outward toward cheek

BEE
(action: a bee stings)
Handshape: 8 changes to open
Orientation: palm left
Location: right cheek
Movement: quickly change to slap cheek with open hand

Sport Signs

Most sport signs and other signs for recreation can be said to be iconic because they show the action of the sport. The following are sport signs with an iconic element.

BOWLING, BOWL

Handshape: curved 3
Orientation: palm forward, fingers pointing down
Location: near right hip
Movement: swing hand forward and upward

BALL

Handshape: C : C
Orientation: palms facing each other
Location: neutral space
Movement: move hands toward each other with a short double movement

BASKETBALL

Handshape: 5 : 5
Orientation: palms apart and facing each other, fingers pointing forward
Location: in front of each side of the chest
Movement: twist wrists upward with a double movement

GOLF

Handshape: A : A
Orientation: RH palm left; LH palm in
Location: RH by right hip; LH across body near right hip
Movement: swing RH up toward the left

FOOTBALL

Handshape: 5 : 5
Orientation: palms down, fingers pointing toward each other
Location: neutral space
Movement: bring hands together with a double movement, interlocking fingers each time

EXERCISE

Handshape: S : S
Orientation: both palms forward
Location: near each shoulder
Movement: move hands upward and outward with a double movement

BASEBALL, SOFTBALL

Handshape: S : S
Orientation: palms facing in opposite directions; little-finger side of RH on index-finger side of LH
Location: in front of right shoulder
Movement: move hands downward across the body

VOLLEYBALL

Handshape: open : open
Orientation: both palms forward, fingers pointing up
Location: near each side of the head
Movement: push hands upward and forward with a double movement

FISHING

Handshape: modified X : modified X
Orientation: palms facing in opposite directions
Location: neutral space; RH forward of the LH
Movement: move back toward chest with a quick double movement

PLAY CARDS, CARDS

Handshape: modified X : modified X
Orientation: palms facing in opposite directions
Location: near each other in neutral space
Movement: move RH off the left thumb with a repeated movement

ROLLER SKATING, SKATE

Handshape: bent V : bent V
Orientation: both palms up, fingers pointing forward
Location: neutral space; RH forward of LH
Movement: move hands forward and back with a repeated and alternating swinging movement

ICE SKATING, SKATE

Handshape: X : X
Orientation: both palms up, fingers pointing forward
Location: neutral space; RH forward of LH
Movement: move hands forward and back with a repeated and alternating swinging movement

BILLIARDS, POOL

Handshape: A : F
Orientation: RH palm back, fingers down, elbow extended back; LH palm right, arm extended forward
Location: RH near right side; LH extended forward
Movement: move RH forward a short distance

HUNTING, HUNT

Handshape: L : L
Orientation: palms facing in opposite directions, fingers pointing forward
Location: in front of chest; LH forward of RH
Movement: downward with a short double movement

HOCKEY

Handshape: X : open
Orientation: both palms up
Location: neutral space
Movement: move RH upward in a circular movement, brushing right index finger on left palm each time

SWIM, SWIMMING

Handshape: open : open
Orientation: both palms down, right fingers across left fingers
Location: neutral space
Movement: bring hands apart with a double movement

BOX, BOXING, FIGHT

Handshape: S : S
Orientation: both palms apart and down
Location: neutral space
Movement: move hands in a repeated circular movement toward each other

WRESTLE, WRESTLING

Handshape: 5 : 5
Orientation: palms facing each other, fingers interlocked
Location: neutral space
Movement: bend wrists downward with a double movement

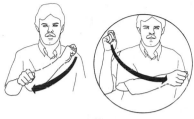

TENNIS

Handshape: A
Orientation: palm left
Location: near left shoulder
Movement: swing hand downward to the right; repeat from near right shoulder

SOCCER

Handshape: B : B
Orientation: RH palm left; LH palm in
Location: RH near right side of body; LH neutral space
Movement: swing the right index finger upward with a double movement against the little-finger side of the left hand

SKIING, SKI

Handshape: X : X
Orientation: both palms up
Location: neutral space; RH closer to chest than LH
Movement: move hands forward

RUN, RUNNING

Handshape: L : L
Orientation: palms facing in opposite directions
Location: neutral space; LH forward of RH
Movement: with right index finger hooked on left thumb,
move hands forward

Time Line

Temporal, or time, aspects of sign language occur
along an imaginary time line that passes through the
body from front to back. Adverbs, indicating time, that
are formed forward of the body and with a forward
movement are typically in the future tense. Signs
made with a backward movement toward the back of
the signer represent past time concepts. And adverbial
signs made with a downward movement, close to the
body, indicate a present time frame.

TIME LINE

PAST   PRESENT   FUTURE

Verb Tense

Verb tense is a grammatical tool used to indicate when an activity occurs. In English, inflections are added to verbs to indicate verb tense. In sign language, a temporal adverb is used to indicate when the activity occurs; the verb does not change. Once a time frame is established, the conversation that follows stays in the same tense until changed. The following signs are adverbs often used to define tense.

TODAY (present)

Handshape: bent : bent
Orientation: both palms up and apart
Location: in front of each side of the body
Movement: move hands downward with a short double movement

NOW, CURRENT, PRESENT (present)

Handshape: bent : bent
Orientation: both palms up and apart
Location: in front of each side of the body
Movement: move hands downward with a short deliberate movement

TOMORROW (future)

Handshape: 10
Orientation: palm left
Location: right cheek
Movement: forward while twisting thumb up

LATER, AFTER A WHILE (future)

Handshape: L
Orientation: palm left, fingers pointing up
Location: right cheek
Movement: forward, ending with index finger pointing
forward

WILL, FUTURE (future)

Handshape: open
Orientation: palm left, fingers pointing up
Location: right cheek
Movement: forward in a double arc while turning the fingers
forward

YESTERDAY (past)

Handshape: Y
Orientation: palm forward
Location: right side of chin
Movement: touch thumb to cheek near chin and then higher on the right cheek

AGO, LAST, PAST, WAS, WERE (past)

Handshape: curved
Orientation: palm back, fingers pointing up
Location: in front of right shoulder
Movement: move hand back over shoulder, ending with palm down and fingers pointing back

Temporal Adverbs

Some signs related to time can be repeated to indicate that something occurs again and again. By signing WEEK with a repeated elliptical movement, the sign becomes WEEKLY. By moving these signs forward into the future or back into the past on the imaginary time line, the sign WEEK becomes NEXT-WEEK or LAST-WEEK.

WEEK, ONE WEEK

Handshape: 1 : open
Orientation: palms facing each other
Location: neutral space
Movement: slide RH from the heel to the fingers of the LH

WEEKLY

Handshape: 1 : open
Orientation: palms facing each other
Location: neutral space; RH above left palm
Movement: move right finger from the heel to the fingers of
the left palm with a double circular movement

LAST WEEK

Handshape: 1 : open
Orientation: both palms up, back of RH on left palm
Location: neutral space
Movement: slide back of RH across left palm from the heel
off the fingers and up toward right shoulder

NEXT WEEK

Handshape: 1 : open
Orientation: palms facing each other, RH on left palm
Location: neutral space
Movement: slide RH across left palm and then upward and forward in an arc

MONTH, ONE MONTH

Handshape: 1 : 1
Orientation: RH palm in, finger pointing left; LH palm right, finger pointing up
Location: neutral space
Movement: slide right finger down the left finger

MONTHLY

Handshape: 1 : 1
Orientation: RH palm in, finger pointing left; LH palm right
Location: neutral space
Movement: slide right finger down the left finger with a double circular movement

YEAR

Handshape: S : S
Orientation: palms facing each other; RH above LH
Location: neutral space
Movement: move RH in a forward circle around LH, ending with little-finger side of RH on index-finger side of LH

NEXT YEAR

Handshape: S changes to 1 : S
Orientation: palms facing in opposite directions
Location: neutral space; RH on top of LH
Movement: move RH forward in an arc while flicking index finger forward

LAST YEAR

Handshape: 1 changes to X : S
Orientation: RH palm in, finger pointing up; LH palm down
Location: neutral space
Movement: bend right index finger up and down with a repeated movement

ANNUALLY, EVERY YEAR
Handshape: S changes to 1 : S
Orientation: palms facing in opposite directions
Location: neutral space; RH on top of LH
Movement: move RH forward while flicking index finger forward with a double movement

Days of the Week

The days of the week are formed in the same position as the manual alphabet, in front of the right shoulder. The signs for the days of the week are the fingerspelled first letter of English word for the day, except for Thursday, which uses the second letter to distinguish it from Tuesday, and Sunday. The sign may be formed with the palm facing forward or back. The following signs for the days of the week show the palm facing back.

MONDAY
Handshape: M
Orientation: palm back
Location: in front of the right shoulder
Movement: small circular movement

TUESDAY

Handshape: T
Orientation: palm back
Location: in front of the right shoulder
Movement: small circular movement

WEDNESDAY

Handshape: W
Orientation: palm back
Location: in front of the right shoulder
Movement: small circular movement

THURSDAY

Handshape: H
Orientation: palm back
Location: in front of the right shoulder
Movement: small circular movement

FRIDAY

Handshape: F
Orientation: palm back
Location: in front of the right shoulder
Movement: small circular movement

SATURDAY

Handshape: S
Orientation: palm back
Location: in front of the right shoulder
Movement: small circular movement

SUNDAY

Handshape: 5 : 5
Orientation: both palms forward, fingers pointing up
Location: in front of each shoulder
Movement: toward each other in a small circular movement

Time of Day

A useful mnemonic device for remembering signs for the various times of the day is to imagine the bent left arm as the horizon. Imagine the right hand to be the sun moving across the sky during the day as shown in the sign DAY. The sign for MORNING shows the sun rising over the horizon, and the sign for AFTERNOON shows the sun going down.

DAY

Handshape: 1
Orientation: palm left
Location: bent right elbow on back of RH of bent left arm
Movement: swing RH down in an arc toward the left elbow

MORNING

Handshape: open
Orientation: palm back; fingers pointing up, LH in the bend of the right arm
Location: in front of right side of body
Movement: raise RH to in front of right shoulder

NOON

Handshape: open
Orientation: palm forward
Location: in front of the right side of the body
Movement: rest the elbow of the bent right arm on the back
of the LH held across the chest

AFTERNOON, MATINEE

Handshape: open
Orientation: palm down; right forearm on back of LH
Location: neutral space
Movement: move RH down with a short double movement

NIGHT, TONIGHT

Handshape: bent
Orientation: palm down; heel of RH on back of LH
Location: neutral space
Movement: tap the heel of RH with a double movement on
back of LH held across the chest

MIDNIGHT, MIDDLE OF THE NIGHT
Handshape: B
Orientation: palm left, fingers pointing down
Location: near right hip
Movement: with left fingers in crook of extended right arm, swing RH to the left

Duration

Duration of an activity is expressed in a number of ways in sign language. One way, used with signs for the time of day, is to form the sign slowly and deliberately to indicate the passage of time. The following signs use large arrows to show duration.

ALL DAY
Handshape: B
Orientation: palm up
Location: bent right elbow near fingers of bent left arm
Movement: swing RH down in a large, slow arc toward the left elbow

ALL NIGHT

Handshape: B
Orientation: palm down
Location: right elbow near fingers of bent left arm
Movement: slowly swing the RH down in a large arc to under the bent left arm

ALL MORNING

Handshape: B
Orientation: palm up
Location: left fingers in the crook of the bent right arm
Movement: slowly swing the RH up in a large arc to in front of the right shoulder

ALL AFTERNOON

Handshape: B
Orientation: palm forward
Location: right elbow on back of hand of bent left arm
Movement: swing the RH down in a large, slow arc

Regularity

One way to express that an activity occurred with repeated regularity, a temporal sign can be held while moving from left to right in front of the body. For the days of the week (e.g., EVERY-MONDAY), the sign is held while the hand moves downward in front of the right side of the body. The following signs show the adverb of regularity.

EVERY MORNING, MORNINGS

Handshape: open : open
Orientation: RH palm up, fingers forward; LH, palm in, fingers pointing right in crook of right arm
Location: in front of left side of body
Movement: swing RH from left to right in front of body

EVERY NOON, AT NOON EVERY DAY

Handshape: open : open
Orientation: RH palm left, fingers pointing up, bent elbow on back of LH; LH palm down, fingers pointing right
Location: in front of body
Movement: move arms to the right in front of body

EVERY NIGHT, NIGHTS
Handshape: open : open
Orientation: RH palm down, fingers pointing forward, heel on back of left wrist; LH palm down, fingers pointing right
Location: in front of the body
Movement: move arms to the right in front of the body

Classifier 1 (CL:1)

A classifier is a handshape used to refer to a noun. The handshape often resembles the referent's size, shape, or some other feature. Classifiers are used to represent the referent and can be used to show the referent's position, movement, or quantity. Classifier 1 (CL:1) is used to represent a person. Imagine the extended finger as representing a person's body. The following signs show the location or movement of a person by using CL:1.

APPEAR
Handshape: 1 : 5
Orientation: RH palm left; LH palm down
Location: right extended index pointing up between index and middle fingers of LH in neutral space
Movement: push index finger straight up

MEET

Handshape: 1 : 1
Orientation: palms facing each other; fingers pointing up
Location: in front of each side of chest
Movement: bring the palm sides of both hands together

CATCH (a person)

Handshape: C : 1
Orientation: RH palm left; LH palm right, finger pointing up
Location: neutral space
Movement: move RH to the left to grasp extended left index finger

RUN AWAY

Handshape: 1 : 5
Orientation: RH palm left, finger pointing up; LH palm down
Location: right extended index finger inserted up between index and middle fingers of LH in neutral space
Movement: pull RH forward

Classifier 3 (CL:3)

Classifier 3 (CL:3) is used to represent a vehicle. First, indicate what kind of vehicle you are discussing, such as a car, bicycle, bus, etc. Then use CL:3 to indicate the movement or location of the vehicle. The speed of the vehicle can be shown by how fast the sign is moved. By forming CL:3 on each hand, the relationship of both vehicles can be shown, such as passing, following, backing up, etc. Here are a few signs using CL:3.

GARAGE

Handshape: 3 : open
Orientation: RH palm left, fingers pointing forward; LH palm down
Location: neutral space; RH under LH
Movement: move RH forward with a double movement

PARK

Handshape: 3 : open
Orientation: RH palm left, fingers pointing forward; LH palm down
Location: neutral space; RH above LH
Movement: tap little-finger side of RH on left palm

HELICOPTER

Handshape: 5 : 3
Orientation: RH palm down, fingers pointing forward;
LH palm right
Location: neutral space; thumb of LH under right palm
Movement: both hands forward while wiggling right fingers

Locational Signs

Prepositions are words that are used to indicate location or the relationship between two or more people or things. Prepositions are always part of a phrase telling more about a noun. Their function in sign language is exactly the same as in English. Prepositions are most easily learned in pairs of opposites. Here are some frequently used prepositions.

ON

Handshape: open : open
Orientation: both palms down; RH above LH
Location: neutral space
Movement: bring palm of RH down across back of LH

OFF

Handshape: open : open
Orientation: both palms down; RH across LH
Location: neutral space
Movement: raise RH a short distance

OVER, ACROSS, AFTER, AFTERWARD, CROSS

Handshape: open : open
Orientation: RH palm left; LH palm down
Location: neutral space
Movement: slide little-finger side of RH across back of LH

UNDER

Handshape: 10 : open
Orientation: RH palm left; LH palm down
Location: neutral space
Movement: move RH from near chest, forward under left palm

IN FRONT OF, BEFORE, FACE TO FACE, FACING

Handshape: open : open
Orientation: palms facing each other and fingers pointing up
Location: neutral space
Movement: move both hands forward a short distance

BEHIND, BACKSIDE

Handshape: 10 : 10
Orientation: palms facing in opposite directions
Location: neutral space, RH in front of LH
Movement: move RH in an arc toward the chest, ending behind LH

TO

Handshape: 1 : 1
Orientation: RH palm down, finger pointing forward; LH palm in, finger pointing up
Location: neutral space
Movement: move right index finger to touch left index finger

FROM

Handshape: X : 1
Orientation: palms facing in opposite directions; right knuckle touching left index finger
Location: neutral space
Movement: bring RH in toward chest

IN, INTERNAL

Handshape: flattened O : flattened O
Orientation: RH palm down; LH palm in; RH above LH
Location: neutral space
Movement: move right fingertips into thumb side opening of LH

OUT, GET OUT, GO OUT

Handshape: 5 changes to flattened O : C
Orientation: RH palm down; LH palm right; right fingers in thumb side opening of LH
Location: neutral space
Movement: bring RH upward closing fingers to flattened O

ABOVE

Handshape: open : open
Orientation: both palms down
Location: neutral space; RH on back of LH
Movement: move RH upward in an arc

BELOW

Handshape: open : open
Orientation: both palms down
Location: LH on back of RH
Movement: move RH downward in an arc

Classifier V (CL:V)

A classifier is a handshape that is used to represent a noun. A classifier can contain information such as size, shape, and type of object. It can also be used to show movement and location. Classifier V (CL:V) represents a person's legs and is used to demonstrate a person's movement or action. Sometimes the fingers are bent as if the person's legs were bent at the knees.

STAND

Handshape: V : open
Orientation: RH palm in, fingers pointing down on left palm; LH palm up
Location: neutral space

JUMP

Handshape: V : open
Orientation: RH palm in; LH palm up
Location: neutral space; right fingers in left palm
Movement: move RH up and down touching fingers to left palm each time

FALL

Handshape: V : open
Orientation: RH palm in, fingers pointing down on left palm; LH palm up
Location: neutral space
Movement: flip RH over, ending with back of RH on left palm

DANCE

Handshape: V : open
Orientation: RH palm in, fingers pointing down; LH palm up
Location: neutral space
Movement: swing right fingers over left palm with a double movement

SIT

Handshape: Bent V : H
Orientation: both palms down, right fingers curved across left fingers
Location: neutral space

LIE, LIE DOWN

Handshape: V : open
Orientation: both palms up, fingers pointing forward
Location: neutral space; back of RH on left palm
Movement: pull RH back toward body

CLIMB, LADDER

Handshape: bent V : bent V
Orientation: palms facing each other
Location: neutral space; LH higher than RH
Movement: with alternating movement, move hands upward

RIDE (a horse)

Handshape: 3 : open
Orientation: RH palm in; LH palm right
Location: neutral space; right fingers straddling index-finger side of LH
Movement: move both hands forward in a double arc

HOP

Handshape: V changes to bent V: open
Orientation: RH palm in; LH palm up
Location: neutral space; RH above LH
Movement: bring right fingers down to hit left palm, with a double movement, bending the fingers each time

Noun/Verb Pairs

There are a series of signs that are made exactly the same, except the movement, which differentiates whether the sign is a noun or a verb. Almost always, the noun had a repeated and restrained movement, whereas the verb is sometimes a single movement and sometimes repeated. Because the differences are not easily memorized by a single rule, it is imporant to watch Deaf people closely to see how they use these signs. Here are a few noun/verb pairs.

EAT

Handshape: flattened O
Orientation: palm down, fingers pointing in
Location: near lips
Movement: move fingers to the lips
Note: Similar to FOOD except made with single movement

FOOD

Handshape: flattened O
Orientation: palm down, fingers pointing in
Location: near lips
Movement: move fingers to lips with a double movement
Note: Similar to EAT except made with double movement

CHAIR, SEAT

Handshape: H : H
Orientation: both palms down
Location: neutral space; right fingers across left fingers
Movement: tap right fingers across left fingers with a double movement
Note: Similar to SIT except made with double movement

SIT

Handshape: H : H
Orientation: both palms down
Location: neutral space; right fingers across left fingers
Movement: none
Note: Similar to SEAT except made with single movement

FLY

Handshape: thumb, index finger, and little finger extended
Orientation: palm down
Location: in front of right shoulder
Movement: forward and upward with a long movement

AIRPLANE, JET, PLANE
Handshape: thumb, index finger, and little finger extended
Orientation: palm down
Location: in front of right shoulder
Movement: forward with a short double movement
Note: Similar tor FLY except made with double movement

CAR, AUTOMOBILE
Handshape: S : S
Orientation: palms apart facing each other
Location: in front of the chest; LH higher than RH
Movement: move hands up and down with short repeated alternating movements
Note: Similar to DRIVE except with a shorter movement

DRIVE
Handshape: S : S
Orientation: palms apart facing each other
Location: in front of the chest, LH higher than RH
Movement: move hands up and down with large repeated alternating movements
Note: Simolar to CAR except with a larger movement

GAS, FUEL, GASOLINE

Handshape: 10 : S
Orientation: RH palm forward, thumb left; LH palm right
Location: neutral space; RH above LH
Movement: twist right wrist to the left with a double movement to dip the right thumb into thumb-side opening of LH
Note: Similar to FILL-UP except made with single movement

FILL-UP

Handshape: 10 : S
Orientation: RH palm forward, thumb left; LH palm right
Location: neutral space; RH above LH
Movement: move right wrist to the left in an arc to dip the right thumb into thumb-side opening of LH
Note: Similar to GAS except made with single movement

OVEN

Handshape: open : open
Orientation: RH palm up; LH palm down
Location: neutral space; LH above RH
Movement: RH slides forward
Note: Similar to BAKE except made with a double movement

BAKE

Handshape: open : open
Orientation: RH palm up; LH palm down
Location: neutral space; LH above RH
Movement: RH slides forward under LH
Note: Similar to OVEN except made with a double movement

Directional Verbs

Sign language is a spacial language, meaning that it occurs in space. Movement and directionality are important factors in its grammar. By moving certain verb signs through space in a particular direction, a singer can indicate the relationship between the subject of the sentence and its object. Here are a few of those verbs that tell by their movement who is the subject and who is the object of the sentence.

GIVE (to another)

Handshape: X
Orientation: palm left
Location: neutral space
Movement: move bent index finger back to the chest in an arc

GIVE ME

Handshape: X
Orientation: palm left
Location: neutral space
Movement: move bent index finger forward in an arc

LEND (to another)

Handshape: V : V
Orientation: palms facing in opposite directions
Location: neutral space; little-finger side of RH on index-finger side of LH
Movement: move hands forward by tipping fingers down

BORROW (lend me)

Handshape: V : V
Orientation: palms facing in opposite directions
Location: neutral space; little-finger side of RH on index-finger side of LH
Movement: move hands toward chest by tipping fingers up

INFORM (another)

Handshape: flattened O changes to 5 : flattened O changes to 5

Orientation: both palms up, fingers angled up

Location: RH near forehead; LH in front of chest

Movement: move hands forward while opening the fingers

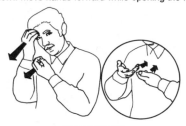

INFORM ME

Handshape: flattened O changes to 5 : flattened O changes to 5

Orientation: both palms up, fingers angled up

Location: RH near forehead; LH in front of chest

Movement: move hands down while opening the fingers

Part Three

At a Restaurant

Quantity

Sign language has several grammatical devices for expressing quantity. One way is to use classifiers that show amounts. Another way is to use an adjective or number expressing quantity either before or after the noun. The following signs are used as adjectives to tell quantity.

MANY, A LOT, NUMEROUS
Handshape: S changes to 5 : S changes to 5
Orientation: both palms up
Location: neutral space
Movement: flick fingers open quickly
Note: This sign may be made with one hand.

TOO MUCH, EXCEED, EXCESS
Handshape: bent : bent
Orientation: both palms down
Location: neutral space; right fingers overlapping left fingers
Movement: move RH up in an arc

ALL, ENTIRE, WHOLE
Handshape: open : open
Orientation: RH palm forward; LH palm in
Location: RH in front of upper chest; LH neutral space
Movement: move RH in large circle around LH, ending with back of RH in left palm

ENOUGH, ADEQUATE, PLENTY, SUFFICIENT
Handshape: open : S
Orientation: RH palm down; LH palm in
Location: neutral space
Movement: push right palm forward on index-finger side of LH

SOME, PART, PIECE

Handshape: open : open
Orientation: RH palm left; LH palm up
Location: neutral space
Movement: slide little-finger side of RH across left palm

FEW, SEVERAL

Handshape: A changes to 4
Orientation: palm up
Location: neutral space
Movement: spread out each finger from the index finger to the little finger

TINY, LITTLE BIT, SCANT

Handshape: modified X
Orientation: palm up
Location: neutral space
Movement: flick thumb upward

MORE

Handshape: flattened O : flattened O
Orientation: both palms down, fingers pointing toward each other
Location: neutral space
Movement: tap fingertips together with a double movement

FULL, COMPLETE

Handshape: open : S
Orientation: RH palm down; LH palm right
Location: neutral space
Movement: slide right palm left across index-finger side of LH

FILL UP

Handshape: B : C
Orientation: RH palm down; LH palm right
Location: neutral space; RH below LH
Movement: bring RH up until level with top of LH

EMPTY, BARE, VACANT, VOID
Handshape: 5, middle finger bent : open
Orientation: both palms down
Location: neutral space; right middle finger on left wrist
Movement: move RH middle finger from left wrist to off the fingertips

Conceptually Accurate Signing

When using sign language, it is important to think of the concept that is being signed, not the English translation. Many words in English sound alike, but have different meanings, such as *run*, which could be used as *run around the block, a run in my hose,* or *your nose may run.* There is a sign for each concept in these three examples even though the English word *run* is spelled the same no matter what the meaning. Here are some other examples.

RIGHT (direction)
Handshape: R
Orientation: palm forward
Location: right side of body
Movement: to the right a short distance

RIGHT (correct), **ACCURATE, CORRECT**
Handshape: 1 : 1
Orientation: palms facing in opposite directions, index fingers pointing forward, RH above LH
Location: neutral space
Movement: hit right little finger on index finger of LH

RIGHT (privilege), **ALL RIGHT, PRIVILEGE**
Handshape: open : open
Orientation: RH palm left, fingers on left palm; LH palm up
Location: neutral space
Movement: slide right little finger across left palm

CALL (telephone), **PHONE** (verb)
Handshape: Y
Orientation: palm left
Location: near right side of face
Movement: bring palm side of RH to right cheek, little finger near mouth and thumb near ear

CALL (yell), HOLLER, YELL
Handshape: C
Orientation: palm left
Location: around right side of mouth

CALL (name)
Handshape: H : H
Orientation: palms angled in opposite directions, right middle finger across left index finger
Location: neutral space
Movement: move hands forward in an arc

FIRE (flames)
Handshape: 5 : 5
Orientation: both palms in, hands apart, fingers pointing up
Location: in front of waist
Movement: move hands upward while wiggling the fingers

FIRE (terminate)**, TERMINATE**
Handshape: open : B
Orientation: RH palm up; LH palm in, fingers pointing right
Location: neutral space
Movement: swing back of RH across index-finger side
of LH

FIRE (shoot)**, SHOOT**
Handshape: L : L
Orientation: palms facing each other, index fingers pointing
forward
Location: in front of chest
Movement: bend index fingers with a double movement

PATIENT (sick person)
Handshape: P
Orientation: palm in
Location: upper left arm
Movement: move right middle finger first down and forward
on upper left arm

PATIENT (enduring), **BEAR, ENDURE, TOLERATE**
Handshape: A
Orientation: palm left
Location: mouth
Movement: move right thumb down to chin

MATCH (verb), **COMBINE, FIT, MERGE, SUIT**
Handshape: bent 5 : bent 5
Orientation: both palms in, hands apart, fingers pointing toward each other
Location: neutral space
Movement: bring hands together to mesh fingers together

MATCH (noun)
Handshape: A : open
Orientation: RH palm left above LH; LH palm right
Location: neutral space
Movement: flick right index-finger knuckle upward on left palm with a double movement left

DRINK (noun)

Handshape: C
Orientation: palm left
Location: near mouth
Movement: keeping the thumb near the chin, tip hand
upward toward the face

DRINK (verb)

Handshape: C
Orientation: palm left
Location: near mouth
Movement: keeping the thumb near the chin, tip hand
upward toward the face with a short double movement

Feeling Adjectives

Some signs that are formed with a 5 handshape
have a bent middle finger. Signs formed with the bent
middle finger often, but not always, express feeling.
Here are a few signs made with a bent middle finger.

FEEL

Handshape: 5
Orientation: palm in
Location: center of chest
Movement: move bent middle finger upward on chest

SICK

Handshape: 5
Orientation: palm in
Location: in front of forehead
Movement: touch the bent middle finger to the forehead

PITY, MERCY, POOR THING, SYMPATHY
Handshape: 5 : 5
Orientation: palms forward; middle fingers bent
Location: neutral space
Movement: move hands forward with a repeated circular movements

EXCITE, EXCITED, EXCITING

Handshape: 5 : 5
Orientation: both palms in
Location: in front of each side of the chest
Movement: move bent middle fingers of both hands in alternating circular movement toward the chest

DELICIOUS, TASTY

Handshape: 5
Orientation: palm in
Location: at the lips
Movement: touch the lips with the bent middle finger and then twist the hand quickly forward

Other Adjectives of Feeling

Of course, there are many other adjectives that express how a person feels that do not have a bent middle finger. Like all adjectives in sign language, the adjectives of feeling may come before or after the noun it is describing. Here are some adjectives that describe how a person feels.

TIRED, EXHAUSTED, FATIGUE, WEARY
Handshape: bent : bent
Orientation: both palms in
Location: each side of the chest
Movement: roll the fingers of each hand downward on the chest

THIRSTY
Handshape: one
Orientation: palm in, finger pointing up
Location: top of throat
Movement: move finger down length of throat

HUNGRY, APPETITE, STARVED
Handshape: C
Orientation: palm in
Location: center of chest
Movement: move hand down on chest a short distance

DISAPPOINTED

Handshape: one
Orientation: palm down
Location: chin
Movement: tap extended index finger on chin

LONELY, LONESOME

Handshape: one
Orientation: palm left, finger pointing up
Location: mouth
Movement: pull side of index finger downward on the mouth

HAPPY, DELIGHTED, GLAD, JOY, MERRY

Handshape: open
Orientation: palm in
Location: chest
Movement: brush palm upward on chest with a circular movement

ENTHUSIASTIC, EAGER, MOTIVATION, ZEAL

Handshape: open : open
Orientation: palms facing each other
Location: neutral space
Movement: rub palms back and forth against each other with an alternating movement

WELL, BOLD, HEALTHY, STRENGTH

Handshape: 5 changes to S : 5 changes to S
Orientation: palms in, fingers pointing up
Location: fingers on each side of chest near the shoulders
Movement: bring hands forward with deliberate movement while closing hands

COLD, CHILLY, FRIGID, WINTER

Handshape: S : S
Orientation: palms apart facing each other
Location: neutral space
Movement: holding arms stiff, shake both hands with a small repeated movement

HOT, HEAT

Handshape: curved
Orientation: palm in
Location: in front of mouth
Movement: twist wrist, throwing hand forward

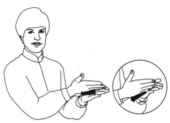

PIE, SLICE

Handshape: B : open
Orientation: RH palm left; LH palm up
Location: neutral space; right fingers touching left palm
Movement: pull right fingers across left palm in several directions

CAKE

Handshape: C : open
Orientation: RH palm down; LH palm up
Location: neutral space; right fingers touching left palm
Movement: pull the right fingers across the left palm in several directions

DESSERT

Handshape: D : D
Orientation: palms facing each other
Location: neutral space; fingers touching each other
Movement: tap fingers together with a double movement

CANDY, SUGAR

Handshape: U
Orientation: palm in, fingers pointing up
Location: chin
Movement: brush fingers downward on chin with a double movement

ICE CREAM

Handshape: S
Orientation: palm left
Location: in front of mouth
Movement: bring index-finger side of hand back in an arc toward mouth with a double movement

POPCORN

Handshape: S changes to one : S changes to one
Orientation: both palms up
Location: neutral space
Movement: alternately move each hand up while flicking out index finger

CHOCOLATE

Handshape: C : open
Orientation: RH palm forward; LH palm down
Location: neutral space; thumb side of RH on back of LH
Movement: move RH in circular movement

VANILLA

Handshape: V
Orientation: palm forward
Location: in front of right shoulder
Movement: shake hand with a small double movement

LEMON

Handshape: one
Orientation: palm left
Location: right side of chin
Movement: keeping index finger on chin, twist hand back with a double movement

APPLE

Handshape: modified X
Orientation: palm down
Location: lower right cheek
Movement: keeping knuckle on cheek, twist hand back with a double movement

ORANGE

Handshape: C changes to S
Orientation: palm left
Location: near right side of chin
Movement: squeeze fingers closed with a double movement

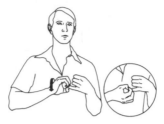

CHERRY, BERRY

Handshape: O : 5
Orientation: RH palm down; LH palm in
Location: neutral space
Movement: while holding left little finger with right fingers, twist RH forward with a double movement

PEACH

Handshape: C changes to flattened O
Orientation: palm left
Location: right cheek
Movement: draw fingers down on cheek and move outward while pulling fingers together

COCONUT

Handshape: C : C
Orientation: palms facing each other
Location: near right side of head
Movement: shake hands

MEAT

Handshape: 5 : open
Orientation: RH palm down; LH palm in
Location: neutral space; bent right index finger and thumb holding index-finger side of LH
Movement: shake hands slightly

BREAD

Handshape: bent : open
Orientation: both palms in
Location: neutral space; right fingertips on back of LH
Movement: move right fingertips down back of LH with a double movement

POTATO

Handshape: bent V : open
Orientation: both palms down
Location: neutral space; right fingertips on back of LH
Movement: tap right fingertips on back of LH with a double movement

CEREAL

Handshape: curved : open
Orientation: both palms up
Location: neutral space; RH in palm of LH
Movement: move RH upward toward mouth with a double movement

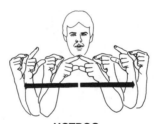

HOTDOG

Handshape: G changes to Baby O : G changes to Baby O
Orientation: palms facing each other; fingers touching
Location: neutral space
Movement: move hands outward while pinching index fingers and thumbs together with a repeated movement

HAMBURGER

Handshape: curved : curved
Orientation: palms facing each other; RH on top of LH
Location: neutral space
Movement: flip hands over, ending with LH on top of RH

SANDWICH

Handshape: open : open
Orientation: palms facing each other; RH on top of LH; fingers pointing to mouth
Location: mouth
Movement: toward mouth with a double movement

SAUSAGE

Handshape: C changes to S : C changes to S
Orientation: palms facing forward; thumb sides touching
Location: neutral space
Movement: move hands outward to each side while opening and closing the hands with a repeated movement

BACON

Handshape: H (thumb extended) : H (thumb extended)
Orientation: palms facing each other; fingers touching
Location: neutral space
Movement: move hands outward to each side while bending the fingers with a repeated movement

VEGETABLE

Handshape: V
Orientation: palm left, fingers pointing up
Location: right cheek
Movement: beginning with index finger touching right cheek, twist hand to touch middle finger to chin

SALAD

Handshape: curved : curved
Orientation: both palms up, hands apart, fingers pointing toward each other
Location: in front of waist
Movement: move hands toward each other in a double circular movement

SPAGHETTI

Handshape: I : I
Orientation: both palms in, little fingers pointing toward each other
Location: neutral space
Movement: move hands in repeated circles

WATER

Handshape: W
Orientation: palm left
Location: mouth
Movement: tap index finger against mouth

MILK

Handshape: C changes to S
Orientation: palm left
Location: neutral space
Movement: squeeze fingers open and closed with a double movement

COFFEE

Handshape: S : S
Orientation: palms facing in opposite directions
Location: neutral space; RH on top of LH
Movement: rub little-finger side of RH on index-finger side of LH with a circular movement

TEA

Handshape: F : O
Orientation: RH palm down, fingers inserted in thumb side of LH; LH palm right
Location: neutral space
Movement: move right fingertips hole formed by LH

SODA

Handshape: 5 changes to open : O
Orientation: RH palm down, bent middle finger inserted in thumb side of LH; LH palm right
Location: neutral space
Movement: pull right bent middle finger from hole formed by LH; then slap right palm on thumb side of LH

BEER

Handshape: B
Orientation: palm left, fingers pointing up
Location: right cheek near mouth
Movement: drag index-finger side down with a double movement

Compound Signs

One type of historical change ASL has experienced is related to fluidity. Signs that were originally two separate signs have combined into a new sign, called a *compound sign*. The transition between the two older signs has become smooth so that only a single sign remains. Compound signs facilitate signing. Here are a few compound signs.

AGREE, IN ACCORD, COMPATIBLE, COMPROMISE, SUIT
Compound Sign: THINK + SAME

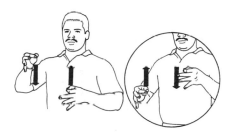

DECIDE, DETERMINE, MAKE UP YOUR MIND
Compound Sign: THINK + JUDGE

BELIEVE
Compound Sign: THINK + MARRY

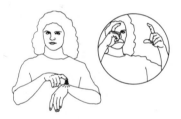

CLOCK
Compound Sign: TIME + shape of clock face

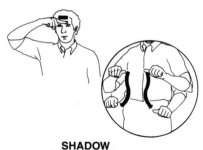

SHADOW
Compound Sign: BLACK + SHAPE

FLOOD
Compound Sign: WATER + water rising

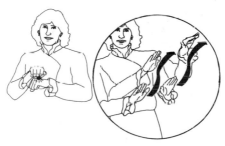

MOUNTAIN
Compound Sign: ROCK + HILL

OCEAN
Compound Sign: WATER + HILL

BREAKFAST
Compound Sign: EAT + MORNING

LUNCH
Compound Sign: EAT + NOON

DINNER
Compound Sign: EAT + NIGHT

ENEMY
Compound Sign: OPPOSITE + PERSON

TOMATO
Compound Sign: RED + SLICE

WATERMELON
Compound Sign: WATER + MELON

PALE
Compound Sign: WHITE + WHITE-FACE

BLEED
Compound Sign: RED + BLOOD

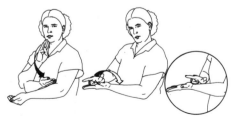

DAUGHTER-IN-LAW
Compound Sign: DAUGHTER + LAW

STEPFATHER
Compound Sign: FALSE + FATHER

ADULT
Compound Sign: OLD + ADVANCED

Thinking and Feeling

Many signs for verbs and adjectives that involve actions or processes of the brain are formed near the forehead. Other verb and adjective signs that involve feelings are formed near the heart. The following are examples of these signs.

THINK, THOUGHTS

Handshape: 1
Orientation: palm down
Location: right side of forehead
Movement: tap forehead with a short double movement

REMEMBER

Handshape: 10 : 10
Orientation: both palms down
Location: RH right side of forehead; LH neutral space
Movement: move RH down to touch left thumb

DREAM

Handshape: 1 changes to X
Orientation: palm down
Location: right side of forehead
Movement: away from forehead while bending the finger

FORGET

Handshape: open changes to 10
Orientation: palm in, fingers pointing left
Location: forehead
Movement. wipe fingers across forehead, changing to 10 hand near right side of head

IDEA

Handshape: I
Orientation: palm down
Location: right side of forehead
Movement: upward in an arc

IMAGINE, MAKE BELIEVE

Handshape: I
Orientation: palm down
Location: right side of forehead
Movement: upward with a double circular movment

WONDER, CONSIDER, MEDITATE, THINKING
Handshape: 1
Orientation: palm down
Location: right side of forehead
Movement: small repeated circle

INVENT, CREATE, MAKE UP
Handshape: 4
Orientation: palm left, fingers pointing up
Location: forehead
Movement: forward in an upward arc

KNOW
Handshape: bent
Orientation: palm down
Location: right side of forehead
Movement: tap fingers on forehead with a double movement

REMIND

Handshape: 10
Orientation: palm up
Location: forehead
Movement: keeping thumb on forehead, twist palm down

MISUNDERSTAND

Handshape: V
Orientation: palm up
Location: middle finger on right side of forehead
Movement: twist hand down to touch index finger to forehead

UNDERSTAND, COMPREHEND

Handshape: S changes to 1
Orientation: palm down
Location: right side of forehead
Movement: flick index finger up with a sudden movement

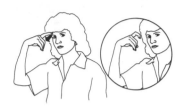

SUSPECT, SUSPICION
Handshape: 1 changes to X
Orientation: palm down
Location: forehead
Movement: pull hand forward with double movement, bending index finger each time

SMART, BRIGHT, CLEVER, INTELLIGENT
Handshape: 1
Orientation: palm left, finger pointing up
Location: forehead
Movement: forward a few inches

DUMB, STUPID
Handshape: A
Orientation: palm in
Location: in front of forehead
Movement: hit palm side of hand against forehead

PREFER, RATHER

Handshape: open changes to 10
Orientation: palm in, fingers pointing left
Location: chest
Movement: pull hand to right while closing the fingers

LOVE, HUG

Handshape: O : O
Orientation: palms in
Location: chest
Movement: with wrists crossed, move palms against opposite sides of chest

FEAR, FRIGHTENED, SCARED

Handshape: A changes to 5 : A changes to 5
Orientation: palms facing toward each other
Location: in front of each side of chest
Movement: move hands toward each other while opening the fingers

PROUD, PRIDE

Handshape: 10
Orientation: palm down
Location: lower chest
Movement: drag thumb upward on chest

WISH, DESIRE

Handshape: C
Orientation: palm in
Location: upper chest
Movement: move fingers downward on chest

DEPRESSED, DISCOURAGED

Handshape: 5 : 5
Orientation: both palms in, fingers pointing toward each other
Location: chest
Movement: pull bent middle fingers of both hands downward on chest

Part Four

Going Shopping

Initialized Signs

An initialized sign is a sign from American Sign
Lanuage formed with handshape from the Manual
Alphabet that corresponds with the first letter of the
English word that is used to translate the sign. The
technique of initializing signs was invented to try to
differentiate between different possible translations of
a signed word. The following signs for colors are most-
ly formed in a similar manner except for the handshape which is initialized.

RED

Handshape: one
Orientation: palm in
Location: mouth
Movement: pull index finger down on lips with a double
movement, bending finger each time

BLUE

Handshape: B
Orientation: palm left
Location: in front of right side of body
Movement: twist hand back and forth

YELLOW

Handshape: Y
Orientation: palm left
Location: in front of right side of body
Movement: twist hand back and forth

GREEN

Handshape: G
Orientation: palm left
Location: in front of right side of body
Movement: twist hand back and forth

PURPLE

Handshape: P
Orientation: palm left
Location: in front of right side of body
Movement: twist hand back and forth

BROWN

Handshape: B
Orientation: palm left, fingers pointing up
Location: right cheek
Movement: pull index finger down on cheek

TAN

Handshape: T
Orientation: palm left, fingers pointing up
Location: right cheek
Movement: pull index-finger side of RH on cheek

BLACK

Handshape: one
Orientation: palm down, finger pointing left
Location: forehead
Movement: drag side of index finger from left to right on forehead

WHITE

Handshape: C changes to flattened O
Orientation: palm in
Location: chest
Movement: pull hand forward while closing the fingers

Classifier F (CL:F)

A classifier represents a noun and is used to show location, movement, and relationship between objects. Classifier F (CL:F) uses an *F* handshape to show the shape of a small round object. The thumb side of the *F* hand can be placed wherever the object is located. The following signs are CL:F signs.

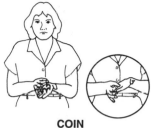

COIN

Handshape: F : open
Orientation: RH palm left; LH palm up
Location: neutral space
Movement: place right curved fingers several places on left palm

BUTTON

Handshape: F
Orientation: palm left
Location: chest
Movement: touch index-finger side of hand several places down center of chest

WATCH (for telling time)
Handshape: F
Orientation: palm left
Location: palm side of RH on left wrist

SPOT

Handshape: F
Orientation: palm left
Location: left side of chest
Movement: place index-finger side of RH on left side of chest

Money

The signs in this part are related to money and shopping. The signs for coins are compound signs that combine the sign for *cent* with the number that tells how many cents. The signs for the amount of money expressed in dollars up to ten dollars is formed by signing the number and twisting the hand back. Other quantities are expressed in the same order as they are spoken using the sign DOLLAR and the sign CENT.

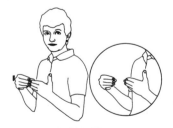

DOLLAR

Handshape: flattened O : open
Orientation: both palms facing in, right fingers holding left fingers
Location: neutral space
Movement: pull RH to the right with a double movement

PENNY, CENT

Handshape: 1
Orientation: palm down
Location: right side of forehead
Movement: forward with a double movement

NICKEL, FIVE CENTS

Handshape: 5
Orientation: palm down, bent middle finger touching forehead
Location: right side of forehead
Movement: forward with a double movement

DIME, TEN CENTS

Handshape: 1 changes to 10
Orientation: palm down
Location: right side of forehead
Movement: forward while changing to 10 hand, then shake 10 hand

QUARTER, TWENTY-FIVE CENTS

Handshape: 1 changes to 5
Orientation: palm down
Location: right side of forehead
Movement: forward while changing to 5 hand, then wiggle bent middle finger of 5 hand

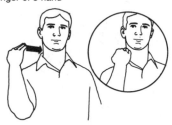

BROKE, PENNILESS

Handshape: bent
Orientation: palm down, fingers pointing back
Location: near right side of neck
Movement: hit little finger against neck with a deliberate movement while bending the neck to the left

MONEY, FUND

Handshape: flattened O : open
Orientation: both palm up, RH above left palm
Location: neutral space
Movement: tap back of RH on left palm with a double movement

SPEND

Handshape: S changes to 5 : S changes to 5
Orientation: both palms up, fingers angled forward
Location: near each side of the body
Movement: move hands up while opening fingers

PAY

Handshape: 1 : open
Orientation: RH palm down; LH palm up
Location: neutral space
Movement: move right index finger from heel to fingers of left palm

PRICE, COST, VALUE, WORTH

Handshape: F : F
Orientation: palms facing each other, fingers touching
Location: neutral space
Movement: tap fingertips together with a double movement

COST, CHARGE, FEE, FINE, PRICE, TAX
Handshape: X : open
Orientation: RH palm in, index finger knuckle on left palm; LH palm right, fingers pointing forward
Location: neutral space
Movement: bring right knuckle down on left palm

CHARGE, CREDIT CARD
Handshape: S : open
Orientation: RH palm left, little finger on left palm; LH palm up
Location: neutral space
Movement: RH hand rubs back and forth on left palm

SAVE, PRESERVE, RETAIN, STORE
Handshape: V : V
Orientation: both palms in, fingers pointing up
Location: neutral space; LH closer to chest than RH
Movement: tap right fingers on back of left fingers with a double movement

SHOP, SHOPPING
Handshape: flattened O : open
Orientation: both palms up; RH above LH
Location: neutral space
Movement: move RH forward with a double movement, brushing back of right fingers on left palm

Numbers

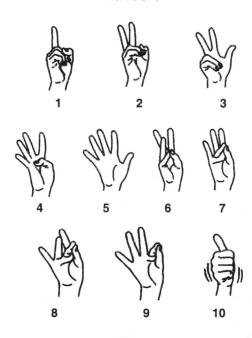

| 1 | 2 | 3 |

| 4 | 5 | 6 | 7 |

| 8 | 9 | 10 |

NUMBER, NUMERAL

Handshape: flattened O : flattened O
Orientation: RH palm in; LH palm down
Location: neutral space; fingertips touching
Movement: twist wrists and touch fingertips together again

ZERO

Handshape: O : open
Orientation: RH palm left; LH palm up
Location: neutral space
Movement: bring little-finger side of RH against left palm

HUNDRED

Handshape: C
Orientation: palm left
Location: neutral space
Movement: move right a short distance

THOUSAND

Handshape: bent : open
Orientation: RH palm down, fingers pointing left; LH palm right
Location: neutral space
Movement: hit right fingertips against left palm

MILLION

Handshape: bent : open
Orientation: RH palm down; LH palm right
Location: neutral space
Movement: hit right fingertips against left palm, first near the heel and then near the fingers

FIRST, ONE DOLLAR

Handshape: one
Orientation: palm forward, finger pointing up
Location: in front of right side of chest
Movement: twist palm in toward chest

SECOND, TWO DOLLARS

Handshape: two
Orientation: palm forward, fingers pointing up
Location: in front of right side of chest
Movement: twist palm in toward chest

THIRD, THREE DOLLARS

Handshape: three
Orientation: palm forward, fingers pointing up
Location: in front of right side of chest
Movement: twist palm in toward chest

FOURTH, FOUR DOLLARS

Handshape: four
Orientation: palm forward, fingers pointing up
Location: in front of right side of chest
Movement: twist palm in toward chest

FIFTH, FIVE DOLLARS

Handshape: five
Orientation: palm forward, fingers pointing up
Location: in front of right side of chest
Movement: twist palm in toward chest

SIXTH, SIX DOLLARS

Handshape: six
Orientation: palm forward, fingers pointing up
Location: in front of right side of chest
Movement: twist palm in toward chest

SEVENTH, SEVEN DOLLARS

Handshape: seven
Orientation: palm forward, fingers pointing up
Location: in front of right side of chest
Movement: twist palm in toward chest

EIGHTH, EIGHT DOLLARS
Handshape: eight
Orientation: palm forward, finger pointing up
Location: in front of right side of chest
Movement: twist palm in toward chest

LAST, FINAL, FINALLY
Handshape: I : I
Orientation: RH palm left; LH palm in
Location: neutral space; RH higher than LH
Movement: bring right little finger downward, striking left little finger as it passes

Adjectives

The order of signs in sentences in sign language is not as strict as word order in English grammar. Adjectives can be signed either before or after the noun, but generally the adjective is signed after the noun. Sign language tends to be topical; that is the primary topic is introduced first and then it is described with adjectives. Predicate adjectives are signed after the verb, just as in English. Here are some adjectives.

TALL, HEIGHT

Handshape: bent
Orientation: palm down, fingers pointing left
Location: near right shoulder
Movement: raise hand upward

SHORT (height)**, LITTLE, SMALL**

Handshape: bent
Orientation: palm down, fingers pointing left
Location: near right side of the body
Movement: move hand downward with a double movement

FAT, CHUBBY

Handshape: curved : curved
Orientation: both palms facing back
Location: near each cheek
Movement: outward to each side a short distance
Note: Puff out cheeks while forming the sign.

THIN, GAUNT, LEAN, SLIM, SKINNY

Handshape: G
Orientation: palm in
Location: in front of mouth
Movement: down a short distance
Note: Suck in cheeks while forming the sign.

LONG, LENGTH

Handshape: 1
Orientation: palm in, finger pointing left touching wrist of extended left arm
Location: in front of the body
Movement: move right finger up the length of left arm from the wrist to the shoulder

SHORT (time), SOON, TEMPORARY

Handshape: H : H
Orientation: palms angled toward each other
Location: neutral space
Movement: rub right fingers back and forth with a short repeated movement on left fingers

DIRTY, FILTHY, SOILED

Handshape: 5
Orientation: palm down
Location: back of hand under chin
Movement: wiggle fingers

CLEAN, NICE

Handshape: open : open
Orientation: RH palm down; LH palm up
Location: neutral space; right palm on of top left palm
Movement: wipe right palm from heel to fingers of LH

UGLY

Handshape: X
Orientation: palm left
Location: in front of left cheek
Movement: move hand to the right while bending the finger

PRETTY, BEAUTIFUL, LOVELY
Handshape: 5 changes to flattened O
Orientation: palm in
Location: in front of face
Movement: move hand in a circle in front of face, closing fingers to thumb in front of chin

HEAVY
Handshape: curved : curved
Orientation: both palms apart and up
Location: in front of each side of body
Movement: bring hands down a short distance

LIGHT
Handshape: 5 : 5
Orientation: both palms facing down, middle fingers bent
Location: in front of each side of the body
Movement: bring both hands upward to in front of each side of the chest while turning the palms up

OLD, ANTIQUE, QUAINT

Handshape: C changes to S
Orientation: palm left
Location: in front of the chin
Movement: bring hand downward while closing the fingers

NEW

Handshape: curved : open
Orientation: both palms up, fingers pointing toward each other
Location: neutral space; RH above LH
Movement: slide back of RH from the fingers to the heel of left palm

WET, DAMP, DEW, HUMID, MOIST

Handshape: 5 changes to flattened O : 5 changes to flattened O
Orientation: both palms in, fingers pointing up
Location: RH chin; LH in front of chest
Movement: move hands downward while closing fingers

DRY, BORING

Handshape: X
Orientation: palm down
Location: left side of chin
Movement: drag index finger from left to right across chin

POOR, PAUPER, POVERTY

Handshape: curved 5 changes to flattened O
Orientation: palm up, fingers pointing up
Location: left bent elbow
Movement: pull RH down with a double movement, closing fingers to thumb each time

RICH, WEALTH

Handshape: S changes to curved 5 : open
Orientation: palms apart and facing each other
Location: neutral space; RH above LH
Movement: bring palms together

STRONG, POWER

Handshape: S : S
Orientation: both palms in
Location: in front of each shoulder
Movement: move hands forward with a short deliberate movement

WEAK, FATIGUE, FEEBLE

Handshape: curved 5 : open
Orientation: palms facing each other
Location: neutral space
Movement: collapse right fingers into left palm with a double movement

DARK, DIM

Handshape: open : open
Orientation: both palms back, fingers pointing up
Location: near each side of head
Movement: down toward each other crossing wrists in front of chest

LIGHT, BRIGHT, CLEAR, OBVIOUS
Handshape: flattened O changes to 5 : flattened O changes to 5
Orientation: palms facing downr
Location: together In front of chest
Movement: up and apart while opening the fingers

DIFFICULT, HARD, PROBLEM
Handshape: bent V : bent V
Orientation: both palms in
Location: neutral space; knuckles near each other
Movement: move hands up and down with an alternating double movement

EASY, SIMPLE
Handshape: curved : curved
Orientation: both palms up
Location: neutral space; fingers near each other
Movement: brush right fingers upward on left fingers with a double movement

Kinship Signs

Signs are said to have a kinship when two signs have identical handshapes, movements, and palm orientations. The only thing that is different between the two signs is the location where the sign is formed. The signs for family members that you have already learned are kinship signs with the male sign being formed on the forehead and the female sign formed near the chin. These pairs of kinship adjectives signs have opposite meanings.

BIG, LARGE

Handshape: open : open
Orientation: palms apart and facing each other, index fingers pointing forward
Location: neutral space
Movement: bring hands apart

SMALL, LITTLE

Handshape: open : open
Orientation: palms facing each other
Location: neutral space
Movement: move hands toward each other with a short double movement

UP, UPWARD

Handshape: 1
Orientation: palm forward, finger pointing up
Location: in front of right shoulder
Movement: move hand up

DOWN, DOWNWARD

Handshape: 1
Orientation: palm in, finger pointing down
Location: in front of right shoulder
Movement: move hand down

OPEN

Handshape: B : B
Orientation: both palms down, fingers pointing forward
Location: neutral space; index fingers touching
Movement: twist wrists to bring hands apart and turn palms toward each other

CLOSED

Handshape: B : B
Orientation: both palms back, fingers pointing upward
Location: In front of each side of chest
Movement: twist wrists to bring index-finger sides of hands together, turning palms down

SAME, ALIKE, AS, LIKE

Handshape: one : one
Orientation: both palms down
Location: in front of each side of chest
Movement: bring index-finger sides of hands together

DIFFERENT

Handshape: one : one
Orientation: both palms down
Location: fingers crossed in neutral space
Movement: bring fingers apart

HIGHER, ADVANCE, ELEVATE, EXALT, PROMOTE
Handshape: bent : bent
Orientation: both palms down, fingers pointing toward each other
Location: in front of each shoulder
Movement: move both hands upward in an arc

LOWER, DEMOTE
Handshape: bent : bent
Orientation: both palms down, fingers pointing toward each other
Location: in front of each shoulder
Movement: move both hands downward in an arc

AHEAD
Handshape: A : A
Orientation: palms facing each other
Location: neutral space; palms sides together
Movement: move RH forward of LH in a small arc

BEHIND

Handshape: A : A
Orientation: palms facing each other
Location: neutral space; palms sides together
Movement: move RH behind LH in a small arc

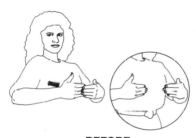

BEFORE

Handshape: open : open
Orientation: both palms in, fingers pointing in opposite directions
Location: neutral space; left fingers on back of right fingers
Movement: move RH in toward body

AFTER, AFTERWARD

Handshape: open : open
Orientation: both palms in, fingers pointing in opposite directions
Location: neutral space; right fingers on back of left fingers
Movement: move RH forward

WIDE

Handshape: open : open
Orientation: palms apart and facing each other
Location: neutral space
Movement: move hands apart to in front of the sides of the body while turning the palms forward

NARROW

Handshape: open : open
Orientation: palms apart and facing each other, fingers pointing forward
Location: neutral space
Movement: move hands toward each other

Symmetry

Many signs use both hands moving independently of each other. These signs almost always have the same hand-shape, location, and type of movement. Sometimes the movement is an alternating movement, with the hands moving in a similar fashion but in opposite directions or one at a time. Here are some signs that follow the rules of symmetry.

JUDGE, COURT, TRIAL

Handshape: F : F
Orientation: palms facing each other
Location: in front of each side of chest, RH higher than LH
Movement: move hands up and down with alternating movements

PARTY

Handshape: P : P
Orientation: both palms down
Location: in front of sides of body
Movement: swing hands from side to side

HOLIDAY

Handshape: 5 : 5
Orientation: palms facing each other, fingers pointing forward
Location: thumbs under each armpit
Movement: tap thumbs under armpits

CELEBRATE, ANNIVERSARY, CELEBRATION, FESTIVAL
Handshape: modified X : modified X
Orientation: palms facing each other
Location: in front of each shoulder
Movement: in circular movements

PLACE, POSITION
Handshape: P : P
Orientation: palms facing each other, middle fingers touching
Location: neutral space
Movement: apart in a circular movement back to touch again near the body

FAST, QUICK, SUDDEN
Handshape: 1 changes to X : 1 changes to X
Orientation: palms facing each other, fingers pointing forward
Location: neutral space
Movement: pull hands to chest while bending index fingers

PERSON

Handshape: P : P
Orientation: palms facing each other
Location: near each side of body
Movement: downward along sides of body

THIN, LEAN, SLIM

Handshape: I : I
Orientation: both palms in, little fingers touching
Location: neutral space, RH above LH
Movement: pull RH up while pull LH down

MONKEY, APE, CHIMPANZEE

Handshape: curved 5 : curved 5
Orientation: both palms in
Location: each side of the body
Movement: pull fingers upward with a double movement

BLUSH, FLUSH
Handshape: flattened O changes to 5 : flattened O changes to 5
Orientation: both palm in, fingers pointing up
Location: near each cheek
Movement: spread fingers open while hands move upward

PANTS, JEANS, SLACKS
Handshape: 5 : 5
Orientation: both palms in, fingers pointing down
Location: on each thigh
Movement: pull hands upward

MANAGE, CONTROL, RULE
Handshape: modified X : modified X
Orientation: palms facing each other
Location: in front of each side of body
Movement: forward and back with an alternating movement

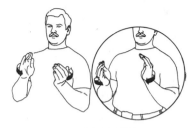

COMPARE

Handshape: curved : curved
Orientation: palms facing each other
Location: in front of each side of chest
Movement: twist hands simultaneously to turn palms toward and away from chest

COMPLEX, COMPLICATED

Handshape: 1 changes to X : 1 changes to X
Orientation: palms down, fingers pointing toward each other
Location: near each side of head
Movement: move hands past each other in front of face while continuously bending finger

TRADE, EXCHANGE, SUBSTITUTE, SWAP

Handshape: F : F
Orientation: palms facing each other, fingers pointing forward
Location: neutral space
Movement: move RH in toward the chest in an arc while moving LH forward

DIRT, GROUND, SOIL

Handshape: flattened O changes to A : flattened O changes to A
Orientation: both palms up
Location: in front of body
Movement: slide fingers of each hand across thumbs

DIPLOMA, DEGREE

Handshape: F : F
Orientation: both palms forward
Location: in front of chest
Movement: move hands apart

DENY

Handshape: A : A
Orientation: 10 : 10
Location: on chest, thumbs pointing down
Movement: drag thumbs downward on chest

DIE, DEAD, DEATH, PERISH

Handshape: open : open
Orientation: RH palm down; LH palm up
Location: neutral space
Movement: flip hands to reverse positions

ACCIDENT, COLLISION, CRASH

Handshape: 5 changes to A : 5 changes to A
Orientation: both palms in
Location: in front of each side of chest
Movement: bring hands together while closing fingers

SHAPE, FORM, IMAGE

Handshape: 10 : 10
Orientation: both palms forward
Location: in front of chest
Movement: bring hands downward with wavy movement

BATH, BATHE

Handshape: 10 : 10
Orientation: both palms in
Location: each side of chest
Movement: rub knuckles up and down on chest with a repeated movement

LIVE, ALIVE, SURVIVE

Handshape: 10 : 10
Orientation: both palms in
Location: each side of chest
Movement: move hands upward

MEET

Handshape: one : one
Orientation: palms facing each other
Location: in front of each side of the chest
Movement: bring hands together in front of chest

TRAFFIC

Handshape: 5 : 5
Orientation: palms facing each other
Location: in front of chest, RH closer to chest than LH
Movement: move hands forward and back with alternating movement

LANGUAGE

Handshape: L : L
Orientation: both palms forward
Location: in front of chest
Movement: move hands apart with wavy movements

CHANGE, ADAPT, MODIFY

Handshape: A : A
Orientation: palms facing each other
Location: neutral space, RH on top of LH
Movement: twist wrists in opposite directions to reverse positions

FINALLY, AT LAST, SUCCEED

Handshape: 1 : 1
Orientation: both palms in, fingers pointing up
Location: near each side of face
Movement: twist wrists to turn palms forward

EXPERIMENT

Handshape: E : E
Orientation: palms forward
Location: in front of each side of chest, RH higher than LH
Movement: move hands in repeated alternating circles

PEOPLE, FOLK
Handshape: P : P
Orientation: both palms down
Location: in front of each side of chest
Movement: move hands in alternating forward circles

Dominant Hand

The signer's preferred hand, whether right or left, is called the dominant hand. According to the grammatical rules of ASL, in a two-handed sign, if only one hand moves, it is the dominant hand and the non-dominant hand remains passive. And if only one hand moves, the hands must have different handshapes. The following signs demonstrate this rule of dominancy.

HELP
Handshape: open : A
Orientation: RH palm up; LH palm right
Location: neutral space
Movement: with little finger of LH in right palm, move RH upward

PRACTICE, TRAIN

Handshape: A : 1
Orientation: RH palm down; LH palm down, finger pointing right
Location: neutral space
Movement: rub right knuckles back and forth on left finger

LIST, RECORD

Handshape: bent : open
Orientation: RH palm in; LH palm right
Location: neutral space
Movement: touch right little finger on left palm, moving from the fingers to the heel

HIT, STRIKE

Handshape: A : 1
Orientation: RH palm in; LH palm right
Location: neutral space
Movement: hit right knuckles against left finger

READ

Handshape: V : open
Orientation: palms facing each other
Location: neutral space
Movement: move right fingers on the left palm, moving
from the fingers to the heel

THAT

Handshape: Y : open
Orientation: RH palm down; LH palm up
Location: neutral space, RH above LH
Movement: bring the right palm down on left palm

SET UP, BASED ON, ESTABLISH, FOUNDED
Handshape: 10 : open
Orientation: both palms down
Location: neutral space, RH above LH
Movement: twist right wrist to move RH in a circular move-
ment down to land on back of LH

LATER, AFTER A WHILE, AFTERWARD
Handshape: L : open
Orientation: RH palm forward; LH palm right
Location: neutral space; right thumb on left palm
Movement: twist RH forward keeping thumb on left palm

AGAINST, OPPOSE, PREJUDICE
Handshape: open : open
Orientation: RH palm in; LH palm right
Location: neutral space
Movement: hit right fingers against left palm

AROUND, REVOLVE, SURROUNDING
Handshape: 1 : flattened O
Orientation: RH palm down; LH palm up
Location: neutral space; RH above LH
Movement: move right finger in a circle around left fingers

MAGAZINE, BROCHURE, PAMPHLET

Handshape: G : open
Orientation: RH palm left; LH palm up
Location: neutral space
Movement: slide right fingers up an down little-finger side of LH

COUNT

Handshape: F : open
Orientation: RH palm down; LH palm up
Location: neutral space; RH above LH
Movement: slide right fingers from heel to fingers of left palm

CLEAN

Handshape: open : open
Orientation: RH palm down; LH palm up
Location: neutral space; RH above LH
Movement: slide right palm from heel to fingers of left palm

TURTLE, TORTOISE

Handshape: A : curved
Orientation: RH palm left; LH palm down
Location: neutral space; LH above RH
Movement: with left palm cupped over RH, wiggle right thumb

START, BEGIN, ORIGIN

Handshape: 1 : open
Orientation: RH palm down; LH palm in
Location: neutral space
Movement: with right finger between left index and middle fingers, twist right wrist

BOTTLE, GLASS

Handshape: C : open
Orientation: RH palm left; LH palm up
Location: neutral space; RH above LH
Movement: move RH upward from left palm

WEAK, FEEBLE

Handshape: bent 5 : open
Orientation: RH palm down; LH palm up
Location: neutral space; RH above LH
Movement: with right fingers in left palm, collapse right fingers with a double movement

RICH, WEALTH

Handshape: O changes to curved 5 : open
Orientation: RH palm down; LH palm up
Location: neutral space; RH above LH
Movement: move RH upward from left palm while opening the fingers

SHINY, GLITTER, GLOSSY

Handshape: 5 : open
Orientation: both palms down
Location: neutral spac;, RH above LH
Movement: move bent middle finger of RH upward from back of LH

SHOW UP, APPEAR, COME UP, OCCUR
Handshape: 1 : open
Orientation: RH palm left;; LH palm down
Location: neutral space; RH under LH
Movement: push right index finger up between left index and middle fingers

AGAIN, REPEAT
Handshape: bent : open
Orientation: both palms up
Location: neutral space
Movement: bring RH up, turning the hand over and touch right fingers on left palm

TIME, PERIOD
Handshape: T : open
Orientation: palms facing each other
Location: neutral space
Movement: move RH in a circle near left palm

Part Five

Let's Practice Signing

Practice Time

In the first four parts of this book, you have learned signs, which are the vocabulary of sign language. Signs are not used in isolation, so it is important to begin to use what you have learned in sentences. In the following section, a short phrase is given at the top of the page. The same phrase is repeated in the box in American Sign Language. Sign the phrase using a sign from the bottom of the page to complete the sentence, substituting a different sign until you can sign the sentence smoothly.

Before you begin, here are a couple more grammatical rules of sign language. The articles, *a, an,* and *the* used in English, are not used in sign language. To sign *the door*, just sign *door*. For all tenses of the verb *to be* (e.g., *am, is, are, was were*), use the same sign *be*, like this:

I sat on _____ .

| I | sit | on |

the bed

a rock

the sofa

the grass

a chair

the floor

The weather forecast is _____ .

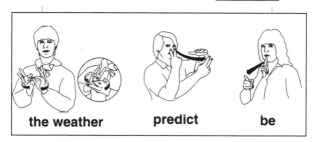

the weather   predict   be

rain   wind

snow   lightning

tornado   flood

The girl has _____ hair.

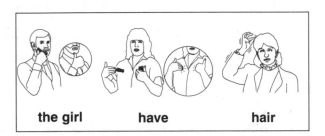

| the girl | have | hair |

black

wet

messy

blond

curly

braided

The man found his _____ .

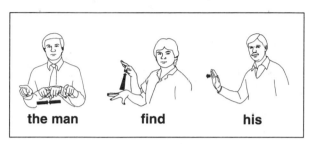

| the man | find | his |

glasses	shoes
book	keys
shirt	newspaper

My job is _____ .

my   job   be

a dentist   a secretary

an attorney   a preacher

a doctor   a waitress

My purse is in_____ .

my purse be in

the kitchen

the car

the drawer

the bathroom

the garage

the store

Turn _____ to go home.

turn   go to   home

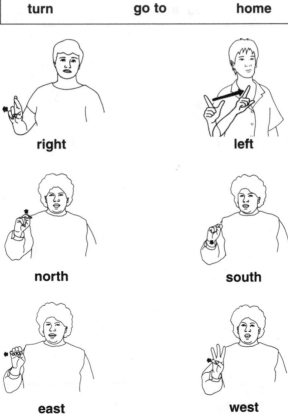

right   left

north   south

east   west

The basket is _____ the table.

| the basket | be | the table |

on

under

behind

in front of

off

below

I saw _____ under the tree.

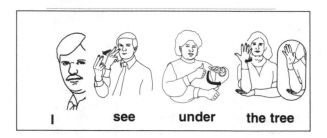

| I | see | under | the tree |

a rabbit

a ball

a squirrel

a dog

a butterfly

a flower

I felt _____ after the movie.

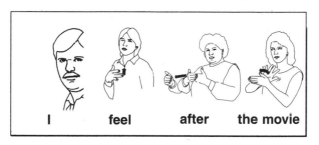

| I | feel | after | the movie |

sad

thrilled

disappointed

satisfied

afraid

happy

The money is in _____ .

the money   be   in

a box   a cup

a pocket   the bank

a bowl   an envelope

Sometimes, my _____ breaks.

| sometimes | my | break |

computer

typewriter

washing machine

copier

zipper

fingernail

We ate _____ for dinner.

we   eat   for dinner

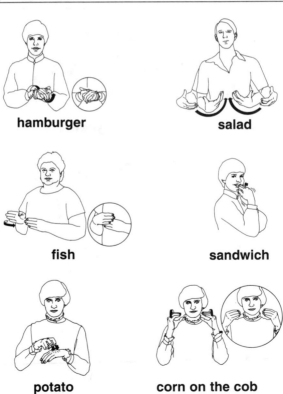

hamburger   salad

fish   sandwich

potato   corn on the cob

Index